CW00521139

TINA TURNER

Biography, Early Life, Career, Social Life, Religion, Legacy, Achievement, Networth, Disabilities And Death Of Queen Of Rock 'n' Roll.

Jesse J. Powers

TABLE OF CONTENTS

INTRODUCTION

Tina Turner was an American-born and Swiss-native singer, dancer, actor, and novelist who passed away on May 24, 2023. She was born Anna Mae Bullock on November 26, 1939. She became well-known as the lead singer of the Ike & Tina Turner Revue before beginning a lucrative solo career, earning her the title "Queen of Rock 'n' Roll" in the process.

In this book, readers will get an intimate look into the life of the Queen of Rock 'n' Roll. This book delves deep into her life, from her early life, to her adulthood, career, family and achievements.

In this book, readers will learn about:

- Her Early life
- Her Career
- How she became popular
- Her Social Life
- Her Net Worth
- Her Death

And lots more

Through resources, friends, family, and sports industry insiders, the author paints a vivid picture of the life of this legendary Queen of Rock 'n' Roll.

BIOGRAPHY

Tina Turner was an American-born and Swiss-native singer, dancer, actor, and novelist who passed away on May 24, 2023.

She was born Anna Mae Bullock on November 26, 1939. She became well-known as the lead singer of the Ike & Tina Turner Revue before beginning a lucrative solo career, earning her the title "Queen of Rock 'n' Roll" in the process.

In 1957, Turner made her professional debut with Ike Turner's Kings of Rhythm. She made her recording debut in 1958 on "Boxtop" under the name Little Ann. With the number-one duet "A Fool in Love" in 1960, she made her solo debut as Tina Turner. Ike & Tina Turner rose to the status of "one of history's most formidable live acts." Before breaking up in 1976, they had singles like "It's Gonna Work Out Fine," "River Deep - Mountain High," "Proud Mary," and "Nutbush City Limits."
Turner began "one of the greatest comebacks in music history" in the 1980s.

The smash song "What's Love Got to Do with It" from her multi-platinum album Private Dancer from 1984 received the Grammy Award for Record of the Year and went on to become her sole song to reach number one on the Billboard Hot 100. She was the oldest female solo artist to reach the top of the Hot 100 at age 44. Her chart success continued with "Better Be Good to Me", "Private Dancer", "We Don't Need Another Hero (Thunderdome)", "Typical Male", "The Best", "I Don't Wanna Fight" and "GoldenEye". She established a then-Guinness World Record for the largest paying crowd for a solo performer (180,000) during her Break Every Rule World Tour in 1988.

Additionally, Turner appeared in the movies Tommy (1975) and Mad Max Beyond Thunderdome (1985).

A biographical movie based on her memoirs I, Tina: My Life Story, What's Love Got to Do with It, was released in 1993. Turner retired in 2009 after finishing her Tina!The 15th highest-grossing tour of the 2000s is the 50th Anniversary Tour. She was the focus of the Tina jukebox musical in 2018.

Turner is one of the best-selling recording artists of all time with over 100 million albums sold globally. Twelve Grammy trophies were given to her, including a Grammy Lifetime Achievement Award, three Grammy Hall of Fame Awards, and eight trophies given in competition. She was the first women and black artist to be on the Rolling Stone cover. She was listed among the 100 Greatest Artists and 100 Greatest Singers of All Time by Rolling Stone. Turner was honored with stars on the Hollywood and St. Louis Walks of Fame.

She was inducted into the Rock and Roll Hall of Fame twice: first in 1991 with Ike Turner and once in 2021 as a solo performer. She also won the Kennedy Center Honors and the Women of the Year award in 2005.

EARLY LIFE

Turner was the youngest child of Floyd Richard Bullock and Zelma Priscilla (née Currie) Bullock when she was born Anna Mae Bullock on November 26, 1939, in Brownsville, Tennessee. She subsequently remembers picking cotton with her family as a young child while they resided in the surrounding rural unincorporated village of Nutbush, Tennessee, where her father worked as an overseer of the sharecroppers at Poindexter Farm on Highway 180. Henry Louis Gates Jr. presented her ancestral DNA test estimates, which were primarily African, about 33% European, and only 1% Native American, when she took part in the PBS documentary African American Lives 2 with him. She had previously thought that she had a sizable Native American background.

Evelyn Juanita Currie and Ruby Alline Bullock, a songwriter, were two of Bullock's older sisters. Additionally, she is Eugene Bridges' first cousin once removed. Bullock went to live with her strict, religious paternal grandparents, Alex and Roxanna Bullock, who were deacon and deaconess at the Woodlawn Missionary Baptist Church, when her parents moved to Knoxville, Tennessee, to work at a defense facility during World War II. Following the war, the sisters relocated to Knoxville with their parents. Bullock attended Flagg Grove Elementary School from first through eighth grade. Two years later, the family moved back to Nutbush to live in the Flagg Grove neighborhood.

Bullock participated in the Spring Hill Baptist Church choir as a small child in Nutbush.

Zelma moved to St. Louis in 1950 when she was 11 years old in order to get away from her abusive relationship with Floyd. In 1952, her father wed a new woman and moved the family to Detroit, two years after her mother had abandoned the family. Bullock and her sisters were transported to live in Brownsville, Tennessee, with their maternal grandmother, Georgeanna Currie. She claimed that her parents didn't love her and didn't want her in her autobiography I, Tina. Zelma had intended to leave Floyd, but after learning she was expecting, she stayed. Turner observed, "She was a very young woman who didn't want another kid."

Bullock served the Henderson family as a domestic helper while still a teen. She was at the Henderson residence when she learned that her half-sister Evelyn and her cousins Margaret and Vela Evans had perished in an automobile accident.

Bullock, a self-described tomgirl, "socialized every chance she got" while attending Carver High School in Brownsville, where she joined the cheerleading squad and the women's basketball team. Bullock moved home with her mother in St. Louis when she was 16 years old after the death of her grandma. In 1958, she earned her high school diploma from Sumner. Bullock took a job at Barnes-Jewish Hospital as a nurse's assistant after graduating.

Tina And Ike Turner

Bullock and her sister started going out to clubs in East and St. Louis. She first caught Ike Turner and the Kings of Rhythm performing live at the Manhattan Club in East St. Louis.

Bullock recalled that she "almost went into a trance" while watching him play, and she was awestruck by his talent. Despite the fact that few women had ever performed with Turner before, she requested him to allow her sing with his band. Turner promised to call her but didn't.

During an interval one night in 1957, she grabbed the microphone from Kings of Rhythm drummer Eugene Washington and began singing the B.B. King's "You Know I Love You" blues ballad. Turner questioned her about her music knowledge after hearing her sing.

She continued to sing throughout the evening and was soon his band's featured vocalist. He instructed her in the finer parts of vocal delivery and control throughout this time.

Little Ann Bullock made her debut recording in 1958 for the single "Boxtop" under that moniker.

Along with Ike and Carlson Oliver, another member of the Kings of Rhythm, she is listed as a vocalist on the song.

Turner wrote "A Fool in Love" for singer Art Lassiter in 1960; Bullock was scheduled to sing background with Lassiter's backing vocalists, the Artettes; when Lassiter did not show up for the recording session at Technisonic Studios, Turner suggested that Bullock sing lead; since Turner had already paid for the studio time, he chose to use her to record a demo with the intention of erasing her vocals and adding Lassiter's at a later date. Murray convinced Turner to make Bullock "the star of the show" and purchased the song, paying Turner a $25,000 advance for the recording and publishing rights.

Turner renamed Bullock "Tina" because it rhymes with Sheena, but her family and friends continued to call her Ann. He based her stage character on Nyoka the Jungle Girl and Sheena, Queen of the Jungle. Turner copyrighted the name and added his last name as a sort of protection so that if Bullock quit like his other singers did, he could hire another "Tina Turner" to take her place.

Early Achievement: 1960–1965

With the release of the record "A Fool in Love" in July 1960, Bullock became Tina Turner. On the Hot R&B Sides chart, it peaked at No. 2, while on the Billboard Hot 100, it peaked at No. 27.

The song was dubbed "the blackest record to ever creep into the white pop charts since Ray Charles's gospel-inspired "What'd I Say" that previous summer" by journalist Kurt Loder. The duo's 1961 single "It's Gonna Work Out Fine" received a Grammy nomination for Best Rock and Roll Performance after peaking at No. 2 on the R&B chart and No. 14 on the Hot 100. The R&B hits "I Idolize You", "Poor Fool" and "Tra La La La La" were all released as singles between 1960 and 1962.

After "A Fool in Love" was released, Ike formed the Ike & Tina Turner Revue, which featured the Kings of Rhythm and a girl group called the Ikettes as backup singers and dancers. As the bandleader, he stayed in the background. Ike pushed the entire revue through a demanding tour schedule across the US, performing 90 days nonstop all over.

The Ike & Tina Turner Revue earned a reputation as "one of the most hottest, most durable and potentially most explosive of all R&B ensembles" during the Chitlin' Circuit era, rivaling the James Brown Revue in terms of musical extravaganza. They were allowed to perform in front of integrated crowds at southern clubs and hotels as a result of their successful performances.

The group recorded a number of passably successful R&B singles between 1963 and 1965 while touring nonstop. The 1964 release of "Too Many Ties That Bind"/"We Need an Understanding" from Ike's label Sonja Records was Turner's debut credit as a solo artist. The pair's "You Can't Miss Nothing That You Never Had" single peaked at No. 29 on the Billboard R&B chart. The duo signed with more than ten labels throughout the course of the following ten years after their time at Sue Records, including Kent, Cenco, Tangerine, Pompeii, A&M, and Minit. They secured a contract with Warner Bros. subsidiary Loma Records in 1964. records that Bob Krasnow owned. Shortly after they departed Sue Records, Krasnow was hired as their manager. With their first charting album on the Warner Bros. label, Live! In February 1965, The Ike & Tina Turner Show reached its highest point at No. 8 on the Billboard Hot R&B LPs chart. Their singles "Tell Her I'm Not Home" (Loma) and "Goodbye, So Long" (Modern Records) both reached the top 40 of the R&B charts in 1965.

Following multiple solo appearances on programs like American Bandstand and Shindig!, Turner's fame increased.whereas the whole revue was broadcast on Hollywood A Go-Go.

After seeing Ike & Tina Turner perform at a club on the Sunset Strip in 1965, music producer Phil Spector persuaded them to take part in the concert movie The Big T.N.T. Show.

Success In The Mainstream: 1966– 1975

Phil Spector was excited to produce Turner because of the group's impressive performance on The Big T.N.T. Show. In an agreement with Ike & Tina Turner's manager Bob Krasnow—who was also in charge of Loma—Spector offered $20,000 in exchange for creative control over the recording sessions for Turner in order to free them from Loma's contract.

In April 1966, after Turner had already recorded with Spector, they signed to the Philles label. The "River Deep - Mountain High" single, their debut on his label, was made available in May 1966. Turner's intense intensity over the "Wall of Sound" on that song was what Spector deemed to be his best composition. It was successful abroad, peaking at No. 1 on Los 40 Principales in Spain and No. 3 on the UK Singles Chart, but it only managed to climb as far as No. 88 on the Billboard Hot 100.

Ike & Tina Turner were chosen as the opening act for the Rolling Stones' UK tour in the fall of 1966 as a result of the record's popularity. Turner made history by becoming the first female and black artist to grace the cover of Rolling Stone magazine in November 1967.

In 1968, the duo signed with Blue Thumb Records, and Outta Season, their debut album, was released in 1969.

Their top-charting cover of "I've Been Loving You Too Long" by Otis Redding was included on the album. They published The Hunter later that year. Turner received a Grammy nomination for Best Female R&B Vocal Performance for the album's title tune, "The Hunter" by Albert King. A range of famous people, including David Bowie, Sly Stone, Janis Joplin, Cher, James Brown, Ray Charles, Elton John, and Elvis Presley, attended the revue's presentations in Las Vegas as a result of the records' success.

Ike & Tina Turner gained popularity in their native country in the fall of 1969 as a result of serving as the Rolling Stones' opening act for their US tour.

Their appearances on The Andy Williams Show, Playboy After Dark, and The Ed Sullivan Show increased their exposure. Come Together and Workin' Together, the duo's two albums from 1970, were both released. Their version of "I Want to Take You Higher" reached its highest point on the Hot 100 at No. 34, although Sly and the Family Stone's original peaked four positions lower.

With the release of the Come Together and Workin' Together albums, they began to veer away from their R&B-heavy sound and integrate more rock songs like "Come Together," "Honky Tonk Woman," and "Get Back."

Their cover of "Proud Mary" by Creedence Clearwater Revival became their biggest hit in the beginning of 1971.

The song sold over a million copies, peaked at No. 4 on the Hot 100, and earned the group the Grammy for Best R&B Performance by a Duo or Group. What You Hear Is What You Get, their live album, was released in July 1971. Their first Gold-certified album was produced at Carnegie Hall. They had a top 40 R&B success with "Ooh Poo Pah Doo" later that year. "I'm Yours (Use Me Anyway You Wanna)," "Up in Heah," and "Early One Morning," their following three singles to reach the charts, all peaked at No. 47 on the R&B chart.

They established Bolic Sound, a recording facility, next to their Inglewood home in 1972. They were put under that label after United Artists Records absorbed Liberty. At this point, Turner started producing more music. The nine out of ten songs on their 1972 album Feel Good were written by her.

With lyrics written by Turner, their 1973 smash single "Nutbush City Limits" (No. 22 Pop, No. 11 R&B) peaked at No. 1 in Austria, No. 4 in the UK, and top 5 in a number of other nations.

The BPI awarded it a Silver certification for selling a quarter of a million copies in the UK. They were so successful that they were given the first-ever Golden European Record Award for selling more than a million copies of "Nutbush City Limits" in Europe. In 1974, "Sexy Ida" and "Sweet Rhode Island Red" were the follow-up hits.

The Gospel According to Ike & Tina, a 1974 album by the couple that received a Grammy nomination for Best Soul Gospel Performance, was released. In addition, Ike received a nomination for his solo song "Father Alone" from the album.

Tina Turns the Country On! is Turner's debut solo record.She was nominated for Best R&B Vocal Performance, Female for her song. Turner shot the rock opera Tommy in London that year. She performed to rave reviews as the drug-dependent prostitute known as the Acid Queen. Turner made an appearance on Ann-Margret's TV special soon after filming was finished. Tommy was followed in 1975 by the publication of Turner's second solo album, Acid Queen. On the Billboard R&B chart, the album peaked at No. 39. It resulted in the hit songs "Baby, Get It On" and a version of "Whole Lotta Love" by Led Zeppelin.

Split: 1976

Ike's cocaine addiction by the middle of the 1970s made it difficult for him to maintain a connection with Turner.

They performed as the opening act at the Waldorf Astoria New York in 1976 and agreed to appear on CBS-TV. Ike made preparations to depart United Artists Records and sign a five-year contract worth $150,000 per year with Cream Records on July 5. The Turners traveled by plane from Los Angeles to Dallas on July 1 to perform at the Downtown Dallas Statler Hilton. On their way to the motel, they got into a fight. Turner sheltered at the Ramada Inn across the freeway shortly after arriving at the motel, running away from Ike with just 36 cents and a mobile card. The divorce was finalized on March 29, 1978, after she filed for divorce on July 27. Delilah's Power (1977) and Airwaves (1978), two more studio albums credited to the group after their split, were made available by United Artists.

CAREER

Her Early Solo Career: 1976–1983

Turner made money in 1976 and 1977 by appearing on TV programs like The Brady Bunch Hour, The Hollywood Squares, Donny & Marie, and The Sonny & Cher Show. Lawsuits for postponed Ike & Tina Turner performances grew after her split from Ike. With money provided to her by United Artists CEO Mike Stewart, Turner started touring again in order to pay off her obligations. Turner made a comeback in 1977 sporting a sexier persona and outfits designed by Bob Mackie. She performed as the star of several cabaret shows at Caesars Palace in Las Vegas and also performed in more intimate settings across the country.

She started her first solo concert tour in Australia later that year.

Turner's third solo album, Rough, was released in 1978 by United Artists with distribution by EMI in North America and Europe. Turner and United Artists Records split after that album and its 1979 follow-up, Love Explosion, which featured a brief detour into disco music, failed to chart. She continued playing and was the star of her second tour even without the expectation of a big song.

After witnessing Turner play at the Fairmont Hotel in San Francisco in 1979, Turner's Australian manager Roger Davies decided to represent her. Early in 1979, Turner worked in Italy as a regular performer on the Pippo Baudo and Heather Parisi-hosted Rete 1 TV program Luna Park.

Later that year, she traveled to South Africa for five weeks during the apartheid era in a contentious tour. Later, she said she was "naive about the politics in South Africa" and that she had regretted her choice.

While at Turner's performance at the Ritz in New York City in October 1981, Rod Stewart extended an invitation for them to sing "Hot Legs" together on Saturday Night Live.

Turner served as the Rolling Stones' opening act in November of that year's American tour. Turner's cover of the Temptations' "Ball of Confusion" for the UK production firm BEF in 1982 became popular in dance clubs around Europe. Turner also sang "Ball of Confusion" on the 1982 album "Music of Quality and Distinction Volume 1" by B.E.F, a side project of Heaven 17.

One of the first black American artists to receive airtime on the channel, she filmed a music video for "Ball of Confusion" that played on the nascent music video channel MTV. Turner made a special guest appearance on Chuck Berry's television show in 1982, which was recorded at West Hollywood's Roxy. A year later, a home video of the concert was made available.

Resurgent Careers And Superstardom: 1983–2000

Turner was regarded as a nostalgia act up to 1983 and performed largely in American clubs and hotel ballrooms. In 1983, she earned a record deal with Capitol Records during her second stay at the Ritz.

She released her rendition of "Let's Stay Together" by Al Green, which was created by B.E.F., in November 1983. It made it to various European charts, including the UK's No. 6 spot. The song's US peak positions on the Billboard Hot 100, Hot Dance Club Songs, and Hot Black Singles were No. 26, No. 1, and No. 3, respectively.

The studio album was approved by Capitol Records after the single's unexpected success. The Private Dancer album, which Turner released in May 1984, took two weeks to record. On the Billboard 200, it peaked at No. 3, while in the UK, it peaked at No. 2. Her most successful album, Private Dancer, sold 10 million copies worldwide and received a 5 Platinum certification in the US. The second single from the album, "What's Love Got to Do with It," was released by Capitol in May 1984.

Bucks Fizz had previously recorded the song. Turner joined Lionel Richie as the opening act on his tour after the album's release.

Turner's song "What's Love Got to Do with It" reached No. 1 on the Billboard Hot 100 for the first and last time on September 1st, 1984. The following singles "Better Be Good to Me" and "Private Dancer" both peaked in the top 10 in the United States. She collaborated with David Bowie on a cover of Iggy Pop's "Tonight" in the same year. It was released as a single in November, and both the UK and the US saw it peak at No. 53.

At the 27th Annual Grammy Awards, Turner completed her return by winning three Grammys, including the Record of the Year Grammy for "What's Love Got to Do with It."

She started her second global tour in February 1985 to promote the Private Dancer album. The NEC Arena in Birmingham, England was used to record two nights of a concert that was eventually made available on home video. She also sang vocals for the USA for Africa benefit song "We Are the World" around this time.

When Turner went to Australia to work with Mel Gibson in the 1985 post-apocalyptic movie Mad Max Beyond Thunderdome, her career flourished further.

She played the glitzy Aunty Entity, the monarch of Bartertown, in the film, her first acting role in eleven years. When she was first released, her performance received mostly favorable reviews. The movie was a worldwide hit, earning over $36 million in the US alone.

For her work in the movie, Turner later won the NAACP Image Award for Outstanding Actress. For the movie, she cut two songs: "We Don't Need Another Hero (Thunderdome)" and "One of the Living," both of which went on to become hits and the latter of which earned her a Grammy for Best Female Rock Vocal Performance. Turner and Mick Jagger both performed at Live Aid in July 1985. When Jagger tore her skirt off during their performance, it startled onlookers. The duet "It's Only Love" that Turner and Bryan Adams released. It received a Grammy nomination, and the best stage performance MTV Video Music Award went to the music video.

Break Every Rule, Turner's sixth solo album, debuted at No. 1 in four nations and sold more than five million copies worldwide in its first year. It was published in 1986.

The United States and Germany alone saw more than a million copies of the record sold. The songs from the album included the Grammy-winning "Back Where You Started," "Typical Male," "Two People," "What You Get Is What You See," and "Two People." Turner had already released her best-selling autobiography I, Tina before the album's debut.

She was awarded a star on the Hollywood Walk of Fame in that year. The third-highest grossing female artist tour in North America that year was her Break Every Rule World Tour, which launched in March 1987 in Munich, Germany. When Turner played in front of roughly 180,000 people at Maracan Stadium in Rio de Janeiro, Brazil, in January 1988, he established a Guinness World Record for the highest paying concert attendance for a single artist at the time.

The Tina Live in Europe CD, which Turner released in April 1988, received a Grammy for Best Female Rock Vocal Performance. She took a break after the tour was over and returned in 1989 with the album Foreign Affair. It debuted at No. 1 in eight nations, including the UK (5 Platinum), where it became her first album to reach that position.

The international number-one single "The Best" was featured on the album, which has sold over six million copies worldwide.

Turner's 1990 Foreign Affair European Tour, which attracted close to four million spectators, broke the Rolling Stones' previous record for a European tour. Simply the Best, Turner's first greatest hits collection, was published in October 1990 and has already sold seven million copies worldwide.

The album is her best-selling item in the UK, where it has sold more than two million copies and earned an 8-Platinum certification.

Ike and Tina Turner were admitted to the Rock and Roll Hall of Fame in 1991. Turner did not go since Ike was in jail and Ike was not present. Following her tour, Turner announced via her publicist that she was taking a leave of absence because she felt "emotionally unequipped to return to the U.S. and respond to the night of celebration in the manner she would want." On their behalf, Phil Spector accepted the honor.

What's Love Got to Do with It, a semi-autobiographical film, was released in 1993. Laurence Fishburne played Ike Turner in the movie, which starred Angela Bassett as Tina Turner.

For their performances, they were nominated for the Best Actor and Best Actress Oscars. Turner contributed to the music for What's Love Got to Do with It, re-recording numerous classic songs as well as some brand-new ones, despite not having a significant role in the movie. Top 10 singles in the U.S. and UK were "I Don't Wanna Fight" and other songs from the soundtrack. Turner started her What's Love Tour in 1993, which largely traveled through North America with a few stops in Australasia and Europe.

Turner made a comeback to the recording industry in 1995 with the release of "GoldenEye," a song that Bono and the Edge of U2 had written for the James Bond movie GoldenEye. Turner's "Wildest Dreams Tour" and the CD Wildest Dreams were both released in 1996.

The dance-infused song "When the Heartache Is Over" from Turner's ninth and final solo album, Twenty Four Seven, was released in September 1999, just before she turned 60. The album was able to get a Gold certification from the RIAA because to the single's success and the tour that followed. With almost $120 million in sales, the Twenty Four Seven Tour had the biggest revenue of any tour in 2000. Turner made her retirement announcement at a concert in Zürich, Switzerland in July 2000.

On December 4, 2005, at a celebration for the Kennedy Center Honors in the East Room of the White House, U.S. President George W. Bush extended his congratulations to Tina Turner. The other awardees are, from left, actor Robert Redford, musician Tony Bennett, dancer Suzanne Farrell, and actress Julie Harris.

Turner's highest charting album in the US, All the Best, which she released in November 2004, debuted at No. 2 on the Billboard 200 albums chart in 2005. Three months after its release, the album attained platinum status in the United States. It also did so in seven other nations, including the UK.

Turner was honored by the Kennedy Center Honors in December 2005 and selected to join a select group of entertainers at the John F. Kennedy Center for the Performing Arts in Washington, D.C.

Turner appeared with Beyoncé at the Grammy Awards in February 2008, marking her return to the public eye. She also received a Grammy for her work on River: The Joni Letters. With the Tina!: 50th Anniversary Tour, Turner set out on her first tour in nearly ten years in October 2008.

Turner published a greatest hits collection to complement the tour. The tour was a resounding success and one of its best-selling itineraries ever. Turner formally ended his performing career in 2009.

Turner's 1989 smash "The Best" returned to the UK singles chart in April 2010, landing at No. 9 in large part thanks to an online effort by Rangers Football Club supporters. Turner became the first female music artist to have a top 40 success in each of the six decades from the 1960s to the 2010s, according to UK chart history.

Children - With Children United in Prayer, the follow-up to Beyond's debut album, reached number one on the Swiss charts in 2011. Turner performed on TV shows in Germany and Switzerland to promote the record.

At 73 years old, Turner was the oldest person ever to appear on the cover of Vogue when she did so for the German edition of the magazine in April 2013. A new collection titled Love Songs was issued by Parlophone Records in February 2014.

Turner revealed in December 2016 that she had been collaborating with Phyllida Lloyd and Stage Entertainment on Tina, a musical based on her life. Adrienne Warren played the lead in the production when it debuted in April 2018 at the Aldwych Theatre in London. In the autumn of 2019, Warren performed in the same role on Broadway.

Turner earned the 2018 Grammy Lifetime Achievement Award, and in October 2018, her second book, My Love Story, was published.

She stepped out of retirement in 2020 to work on a remix of "What's Love Got to Do with It" with Norwegian producer Kygo. She made history by being the first artist with a top 40 hit in the UK for seven straight decades with the release of this song.

Turner's third book, Happiness Becomes You: A Guide to Changing Your Life for Good, was published in 2020. Together with Swiss vocalist Regula Curti and American novelist Taro Gold, she co-wrote the book. The editors of Amazon selected it as one of the year's top nonfiction books. Turner made an appearance in the T.J. Martin and Dan Lindsay documentary Tina in 2021.

SOCIAL LIFE

Marriages And Relations

Harry Taylor

Turner (then known as Anna Mae Bullock) originally fell in love with **Harry Taylor** when she was still living in Brownsville. At a high school basketball match, they first met. Initially, Taylor went to a different school, but he moved to the area to be close to her. When she learned that Taylor had married another woman who was carrying his kid, their relationship ended, she admitted to Rolling Stone in 1986: "Harry was really popular and had tons of girlfriends, but eventually I got him, and we went steady for a year."

Bullock and her sister Alline got to know Ike Turner's Kings of Rhythm after relocating to St. Louis. Bullock started dating the band's saxophone Raymond Hill while Alline was dating the drummer Eugene Washington. Turner moved in with Hill, who shared an apartment with Ike Turner, after discovering she was pregnant during her final year of high school. Bullock recalled, "I didn't love him as much as I'd loved Harry, but he was good-looking. I thought, 'My baby's going to be beautiful.'" Their marriage ended when Hill broke his ankle while wrestling singer Carlson Oliver of the Kings of Rhythm, and Hill returned to his hometown of Clarksdale before Bullock gave birth to their son Craig in August 1958.

Ike Turner

They were platonic friends from the time they met in 1957 until 1960. Their affair started while Ike was with his live-in girlfriend Lorraine Taylor. They had sex when she went to sleep with him after another musician threatened to enter her room. Turner compared their early relationship to that of a "brother and sister from another lifetime."

Turner recalled that this incident was the first time he "instilled fear" in her, but she decided to stay with him because she "really did care about him." After the birth of their son Ronnie in October 1960, they moved to Los Angeles in 1962 and married in Tijuana. In 1963, Ike bought a house in Los Angeles. In 1964, Turner moved out of Ike's house and into a hotel.

She had initially been head over heels for him. See what he accomplished for her. Ike was utterly unpredictable, yet it was eventually discovered that he had bipolar disorder.

On July 1, 1976, Turner unexpectedly left Ike after they got into a disagreement on their way to the Dallas Statler Hilton. She dashed across the freeway to the Ramada Inn with only 36 cents and a Mobil credit card in her pocket. Turner filed for divorce on July 27 due to irreconcilable differences.

Her divorce petition requested $4,000 in alimony per month, $1,000 in child support per month, and custody of her sons Craig and Ronnie. On March 29, 1978, the divorce was finalized. Turner accepted responsibility for missed concert dates as well as an IRS lien in the final divorce order.

Turner retained songwriter earnings from songs she wrote, but Ike received publication income for both his and her creations. She kept her two Jaguar cars, furs, and jewels, as well as her stage identity.

Turner granted Ike a portion of their Bolic Sound recording studio, publishing companies, and real estate, while retaining ownership of their four automobiles. Several promoters lost money and filed lawsuits to recover their losses. She received food assistance and played in local clubs to pay off debts for over two years.

They had a common-law marriage and still had to go through a formal divorce, but Ike Turner claimed on numerous occasions that he was never legally married to Turner because he was legally married to another woman at the time of their ceremony.

He also claimed that her birth name was Martha Nell Bullock (not Anna Mae Bullock), even though she signed her legal name as Martha Nell Turner on numerous contracts.

Ike Turner wrote in his autobiography Takin' Back My Name, "Sure, I've smacked Tina. During our battles, I occasionally punched her to the ground without thinking. Roseanne Barr encouraged Ike to publicly apologize to Turner in a 1999 appearance on The Roseanne Show. In 2007, Ike told Jet that he still loved her and that he had prepared a letter apologizing for "putting her and the kids through that kind of stuff," but he had never sent it.

In a brief statement following his passing on December 12, 2007, Turner said: "Tina hasn't spoken to Ike in more than 30 years.

Phil Spector insulted Tina Turner during the funeral, which Turner's sister Alline attended since she still viewed Ike as her brother-in-law.

Robert Bach

Erwin Bach, a German music executive who was over sixteen years Turner's junior and was born on January 24, 1956 in Cologne, Germany, was sent by her European record label (EMI) to meet Turner at Düsseldorf Airport in 1986. Initially friends, they started dating later that year, and in July 2013, after a 27-year relationship, they were married in a civil ceremony on the shores of Lake Zurich in Küsnacht, Switzerland.

Children

She also adopted two of Ike Turner's children, raising them as her own. Turner was 18 years old when she gave birth to her eldest son, whose biological father was Kings of Rhythm saxophonist Raymond Hill. Ike Turner adopted Raymond Craig Hill, and changed his name to Craig Raymond Tu. Turner had two biological sons: one with Raymond Hill, named Raymond Craig, born on August 20, 1958, and the other with Ike Turner, Ronald "Ronnie" Renelle Turner, born on October

Through him, Turner had two grandchildren. Ronnie, the younger son of Turner, was married to French singer Afida Turner and played bass guitar in a band called Manufactured Funk with songwriter and musician Patrick Moten.

Ronnie passed away from complications from colon cancer in December 2022.

Ike Turner Jr. worked as a sound engineer at Bolic Sound and briefly for Turner after her divorce, later winning a Grammy Award for producing his father's album Risin' with the Blues. During Turner's divorce trial, Ike sent their four sons to live with Turner and gave her money for one month's rent. He toured with former Ikette Randi Love as Sweet Randi Love and the Love Thang Band.

RELIGION

Turner once described herself as a "Buddhist-Baptist," alluding to her upbringing in the Baptist church where her father served as a deacon and her later conversion to Buddhism as an adult. In a 2016 interview with Lion's Roar magazine, Turner said, "I consider myself a Buddhist." The February 15, 1979, issue of Jet magazine featured Turner with her Buddhist altar on the cover. Turner has given credit to the Liturgy of Nichiren Daishonin and So

Turner claimed in her 1986 autobiography I, Tina that Ike Turner's friend Valerie Bishop introduced her to Nichiren Buddhism and taught her the chant nam-my-h-renge-ky in 1973.

Turner later claimed in her 2020 spiritual memoir Happiness Becomes You that it was her son Ronnie Turner who first suggested she might benefit from chanting. We are taught how to sing it in the Soka Gakkai tradition. It is a sound and a rhythm that appeals to a part of you. The subconscious mind is the location we seek. Dramatizations of Turner chanting were featured in the 2021 documentary film Tina as well as the 1993 documentary What's Love Got to Do with It.

On August 2, 2005, in Einsiedeln, Switzerland, Turner had a meeting with the 14th Dalai Lama Tenzin Gyatso. She also had a meeting with the Swiss-Tibetan Buddhist vocalist Dechen Shak-Dagsay. In 2009, she co-created the spiritual music project Beyond with Shak-Dagsay and the Swiss singer Regula Curti.

LEGACY

Turner is frequently referred to as "The Queen of Rock and Roll" and is regarded as one of the greatest singers of all time. Journalist Kurt Loder stated that Turner's voice combined "the emotional force of the great blues singers with a sheer, wallpaper-peeling power that seemed made to order for the age of amplification."

Turner catapulted herself to the forefront of a musical revolution that had long overlooked the pioneering contributions of African American women, navigating and reflecting back the technological innovations of a new pop-music era in the 1960s and 1970s, and then remade herself at an age when most pop musicians were hitting the oldies circuit, combining sound and movement at a crucial turning point in rock history.

ACHIEVEMENTS, HONORS, AND AWARDS

Turner formerly held the record for the biggest paid audience for a single act (180,00 in 1988). Turner had 35 UK top 40 songs in total, making her the first artist to do it in seven successive decades. She has sold over 100 million albums globally, including 10 million certified RIAA album sales.

She shares the record for the most awards given for Best Female Rock Vocal Performance with Pat Benatar (12 Grammy Awards total), and three of her recordings— "River Deep - Mountain High" (1999), "Proud Mary" (2003), and "What's Love Got to Do with It" (2012)—are in the Grammy Hall of Fame.

The only female performer to get a Grammy in the pop, rock, and R&B categories was Turner. 2018 saw Turner win a Grammy Lifetime Achievement Award. Turner also received Grammy awards for his performances at the 1986 Prince's Trust concert and as a member of USA for Africa.

Turner was honored with two Walk of Fame stars, one in St. Louis in 1991 and one in Hollywood in 1986. She and Ike Turner were inducted into the Rock & Roll Hall of Fame together in 1991.

Turner was awarded the coveted Kennedy Center Honors in 2005. Several artists paid tribute to her that night, including Melissa Etheridge (performing "River Deep - Mountain High"), Queen Latifah (performing "What's Love Got to Do with It"), Beyoncé (performing "Proud Mary"), and Al Green (performing "Let's Stay Together").

President George W. Bush praised her "natural skill, the energy and sensuality," and called her legs "the most famous in show business." We don't need another hero; instead, Oprah Winfrey said, "Tina, you make me proud to spell my name w-o-m-a-n."

Turner was given a solo induction into the Rock & Roll Hall of Fame in 2021 by Angela Bassett. It's Only Love by Keith Urban and H.E.R., What's Love Got to Do with It by Mickey Guyton, and River Deep - Mountain High by Christina Aguilera were the songs performed.

Turner Also Holds The Following Accolades:

- 1967 saw Turner become the first female and black artist to appear on the cover of Rolling Stone (Issue No. 2).

- **1993**: Turner received the Legend Award at the World Music Awards.

- Turner received the Living Legend Award at the 1993 Essence Awards.

- The French minister of education awarded Turner the Légion d'Honneur in 1996.

- On VH1's selection of the 100 Greatest Women in Rock and Roll from 1999, Turner came in at number two.

- 2002 saw the renaming of Tennessee State Route 19 as the "Tina Turner

Highway" between Brownsville and Nutbush.

- **Proud Mary:** The Best of Ike & Tina Turner was ranked No. 212 by Rolling

  Stone in 2003 on their list of the 500 Greatest Albums of All Time (No. 214 on the 2012 revised edition).

- **2004**: Her rendition of "What's Love Got to Do With It" from 1985 was named one of the top 10 Grammy moments by People.

- In 2008, Turner was voted No. 17 on Rolling Stone's list of the 100 greatest singers ever.

- **2009**: Her rendition of "What's Love Got to Do With It" from 1985 was named one of the top 10 Grammy moments by Time.

- In 2010, Turner was voted No. 63 on Rolling Stone's list of the 100 Greatest Artists of All Time.

- Turner, who was 73 years old, covered Vogue Germany in 2013, surpassing Meryl Streep, who was 62 at the time and had covered American Vogue in 2012.

- Turner was admitted to the Soul Music Hall of Fame in 2014.

- Ike and Tina Turner were voted No. 2 on Rolling Stone's list of the 20 greatest duos of all time in 2015.

- 2015 saw the St. Louis Classic Rock Hall of Fame induct Ike & Tina Turner.

- **2016**: The album Everything You've Come to Expect by The Last Shadow Puppets has a cover with a photograph of Turner taken by Jack Robinson in 1969.

- Turner was honored by the Memphis Music Hall of Fame in 2019.

- 2020 saw the addition of Private Dancer to the Library of Congress' National Recording Registry.

- Turner was inducted into the Rock and Roll Hall of Fame twice in 2021.

- Turner was awarded an honorary doctorate for her "unique musical and artistic life's work" in 2021 by the University of Bern's Faculty of Philosophy and History.

- In 2022, Mattel created a Barbie doll in the image of Tina Turner to celebrate the release of her song "What's Love Got To Do With It."

NETWORTH

One of the all-time best-selling recording artists is Tina Turner. She broke more than 200 million records over her career. She was renowned for having a long career and having powerful vocals.

She was the recipient of 12 Grammy Awards, including a Grammy Lifetime Achievement Award and THREE Grammy Hall of Fame Awards. Tina ended her career as a performer in 2009. In October 2021, Tina, dubbed the "Queen of Rock and Roll," was admitted into the Rock and Roll Hall of Fame.

For $50 million in 2021, Tina sold BMG Rights Management the rights to her music, likeness, and image.

After nearly 30 years of renting in Switzerland, Erwin and Tina were able to purchase a home in 2021 after both of them had finally obtained Swiss citizenship. The couple spent an estimated $76 million in December 2021 for a brand-new lakefront house on the shores of Lake Zurich.

As an American-born Swiss singer and songwriter, Tina Turner had a $250 million fortune at the time of her passing.

DISABILITY AND DEATH

Turner acknowledged having many life-threatening illnesses in her 2018 memoir My Love Story. She had a stroke in 2013, three weeks after getting married to Erwin Bach, and had to retrain her legs to walk. She was given an intestinal cancer diagnosis in 2016. Turner decided to treat her high blood pressure with homeopathic medications. Her high blood pressure caused damage to her kidneys, which ultimately led to renal failure. She was advised to begin dialysis because the likelihood of her acquiring a kidney was slim. She joined Exit and considered assisted suicide, but Bach offered to give a kidney for her transplant. On April 7, 2017, Turner underwent kidney transplant surgery.

Turner passed away in her home in Küsnacht, Switzerland, on May 24, 2023, at the age of 83, after a protracted illness that included cancer, strokes, and kidney failure in her later years.

Printed in Great Britain
by Amazon